Coloring San Diego Landmarks

By Nancy Hendrickson

Sunbelt Publications
San Diego, California

Coloring San Diego Landmarks

Sunbelt Publications, Inc.
Copyright © 2016 by Nancy Hendrickson
All rights reserved. First edition 2016

Cover and book design by Kristina Filley
Project management by Deborah Young

Printed in the United States of America

Sunbelt Publications, Inc.
P.O. Box 191126
San Diego, CA 92159-1126
(619) 258-4911, fax: (619) 258-4916
www.sunbeltpublications.com

18 17 16 15 14   5 4 3 2 1

ISBN: 978-1-941384-25-1

All photography by the author unless otherwise noted.

A Coloring Book Introduction:

Visitors who come to San Diego to enjoy the year-round sunshine quickly fall in love with the city's ambience and charm. While the first stop for many may be the world-famous Zoo, San Diego is dotted with dozens of landmarks that mirror both its Spanish and sea-faring heritage.

Discovered by explorer Juan Cabrillo in 1542, the Spanish influence is seen throughout the city in both art and architecture. San Diego boasts the first of California's 22 missions, making the city the Birthplace of California. The Mission San Diego de Alcalá, founded in 1769, is but one of the landmarks you'll find in this coloring book.

If you're drawn to the water, you'll recognize other images in this book from the San Diego Maritime Museum to Seaport Village, or surfers riding the waves off Mission Beach.

Fancy a stroll in the park? Then head to Balboa Park, located in the center of the city. The Colonial Spanish architecture of the buildings was designed for the 1915 Panama-California Exposition. If you're looking for something more modern, walk over to the Air and Space Museum or the Old Globe Theater complex. We're betting that the breathtaking tile work on the park's California Tower will be one of the first images you choose to color.

If exploring Old Town is high on your must-see list, don't miss the 1827 Casa de Estudillo or San Diego's most haunted house—the Whaley House. You can walk back in history several days a week as period-style blacksmiths ply their trade and Spanish señoritas stroll through the plaza. Of course if you're in the city at Halloween, you'll be treated to the Spanish celebration of the Day of the Dead.

Wherever you choose to go in San Diego you're sure to find at least a few of the 40 of the most iconic San Diego scenes in this coloring book. Choose any one that appeals to you, or pick the landmarks you've just visited. If you live in San Diego, we're hoping the images here will prompt you to revisit the landmarks that make the city so unique.

The pages are printed one-sided on a nice heavyweight paper, so use whatever medium you like to color the images, whether it be crayons, colored pencils, or pens. Once you've completed an image feel free to remove it from this book to frame as a reminder of the days you spent exploring America's Finest City.

Little Italy

Little Italy is located in the northwest section of downtown only a few blocks from the harbor. It was originally settled by Italian fishermen who worked in the city's once-booming tuna industry. It is now home to galleries, upscale eateries, and a thriving farmer's market. Visit this favorite section of the city any night of the week for authentic Italian cooking, local wine tasting, or outdoor dining and people-watching. At least two of the Italian restaurants here have been serving diners for more than 50 years, making them a favorite of both locals and visitors.

Surfing Madonna

The Surfing Madonna is a 10' x 10' mosaic created by artist Mark Patterson that is located in Encinitas, California. It depicts the Virgin of Guadalupe riding a white surfboard with her green robe flowing in the wind. It was originally installed on a roadway underpass without official sanction. The City of Encinitas considered it to be graffiti and ordered its removal. After remaining in storage for a period of time, it was eventually re-installed on a wall of a local business across the street from its original location. The Surfing Madonna inspired the creation of a non-profit organization called Surfing Madonna Oceans Project, which is dedicated to raising money in support of ocean and humanitarian programs.

Surfer

You'll find surfers in San Diego year-round riding the waves at favorite spots including Sunset Cliffs, Black's Beach, South Mission Beach, Ocean Beach Pier, and Swami's—a nickname for a stretch of surf that lies below the grounds of the Self-Realization Fellowship in Encinitas. Surfers have been enjoying the waves here since the early 1900s when big boards reigned supreme. Take a drive along Highway 101 where you'll never fail to see an ocean filled with surfers hoping to catch the perfect wave.
Surfer image derived from photo in Creative Commons attribution
https://www.flickr.com/photos/bnsurf/2070381464

Self-Realization Fellowship

The Self-Realization Fellowship compound is topped with a gold dome and perched on a piece of land in Encinitas just a stone's throw from the Pacific Ocean. The temple is part of a religious organization founded in 1920 by Paramahansa Yogananda. Visitors are welcome to attend inspirational services or stroll the grounds of the meditation garden. Here you'll find koi ponds, spectacular ocean views, meditation nooks, and a wide diversity of beautiful plants. An adjacent chapel is open for daily meditation while retreat programs are offered for those who want to delve more deeply into the teachings of the temple's founder.

Koala

A favorite among San Diego Zoo visitors are the koalas located in the Koala Care Center. The cuddly critters have been delighting Zoo visitors since the first pair—Snugglepot and Cuddlepie—arrived in 1925. The Zoo is proud to have the largest koala colony and successful breeding program outside of Australia. Although often referred to as "bears," koalas are actually marsupials, which is the same group that contains kangaroos and opossums. Koalas are natives of southeastern and eastern Australia and live in eucalyptus trees where they spend their time either sleeping or munching on eucalyptus leaves.

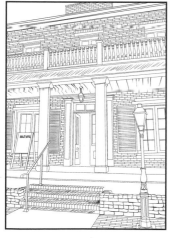

Day of the Dead

San Diego's Old Town swings into high gear during the Dia de Muertos—Day of the Dead—celebration. This multi-day holiday is a time for family and friends to pray for and remember those who are no longer living. Originally it was observed in summer, and over centuries of time, it is now associated with Halloween. Old Town's celebration of the Day of the Dead in the Mercado is November 1 and 2. Festivities are designed to honor the area's history and cultural heritage. Day of the Dead art work abounds with skeletons, flowers, skulls, and other ghostly masks.

Whaley House

The Whaley House on San Diego Avenue in Old Town is the most haunted house in San Diego and is a favorite of ghost hunters from around-the-world. The house was built by merchant Thomas Whaley and was the first two-story brick building in San Diego. The building's long history includes being used as a residence, theater, and courthouse. Even from the early days of the house, tales of ghostly footsteps, specters, and full-bodied apparitions were widespread. Ghost hunting tours are offered here late at night by Museum staff and members of the San Diego Ghost Hunters.

Old Town Trolley

First-time visitors to San Diego can enjoy a great introduction to America's Finest City by spending a day on one of the Old Town Trolleys as it takes them on a sightseeing tour of the city. Visitors can avoid the hassle of parking while spending as much time as desired at any of the Trolley stops. The policy of unlimited reboarding allows riders to hop on-and-off at any of their favorite spots along the route. Stops include Balboa Park, Petco Park, Hotel del Coronado, the waterfront, and the San Diego Zoo.

Seaport Village Carousel

A favorite at Seaport Village is the colorful Looff carousel that was built in 1895. Children and adults can choose their ride from any of the 54 hand-carved animals, including horses, dogs, elephants, and sea monsters. For a less fanciful ride, you can also choose one of the two horse-drawn carriages. The carousel was designed by Charles Looff, who was the most successful of the Coney Island carousel builders. Looff remained a model for new carousel builders as he changed his styles to keep ahead of his competition. The carousel at Seaport Village represents one of his earliest styles while a later style can be found in downtown Spokane, Washington.

Friendship Bell

At the end of Shelter Island you'll find the Friendship Bell housed in a pagoda-like structure designed by Japanese artist Masahiko Katori. The bronze bell was a gift from the citizens of Yokohama, Japan, to their San Diego sister city. The six-foot-high bell is inscribed "Bell of Friendship" in both English and Japanese. There is no inside clapper. It is designed in a traditional Japanese fashion whereby it is rung by being struck with a large wooden ram in the bell house. The Tunaman's Memorial is also located on Shelter Island. It is a larger-than-life bronze sculpture dedicated to the men who served in San Diego's tuna fleet.

Giant Panda

The first giant pandas came to the San Diego Zoo for a 100-day visit from China in 1987. They were such a hit that San Diegans hoped they would become a permanent fixture. In 1996, an agreement was made with China to house two adult pandas and their young offspring here in San Diego. Today, the Zoo has three giant pandas, Gao Gao, Bai Yun, and their cub Xiao Liwu. Panda cubs are returned to China sometime after their third birthday, per the agreement. The trio of endangered species occupies a large natural habitat with trees, climbing structures, and air-conditioned bedrooms. Their home in the wild is in damp areas at elevations of 4,000 to 11,000 feet.

USS Dolphin

The USS *Dolphin*, docked alongside the Berkeley Ferry, is part of the ever-growing collection of the San Diego Maritime Museum. The Dolphin is used for deep ocean research and is the deepest diving submarine in the world. One of the museum's most prized holdings is the *Star of India*, which is docked on the opposite side of the Berkeley Ferry. It is the world's oldest active sailing ship and was built in 1863. The Star had a long career transporting emigrants to New Zealand and later in the Alaskan packing trade. Other popular ships at the Maritime Museum include a Russian submarine and a replica of an 18th century Royal Navy frigate.

Santa Fe Depot

This elegant train depot is located just blocks from the cruise ship piers in the heart of downtown. It was built in Mission Revival style to reflect the city's Spanish Colonial culture and history. The Depot was opened in time to celebrate the city's 1915 California-Panama Exhibition. Among the Depot's features are tiled domes, a massive arch, and twin towers. Interior highlights include a natural redwood beam ceiling and walls of colorful Mexican tiles.

Villa Montezuma

Villa Montezuma is one of San Diego's famous haunted houses. The house is a breathtaking Queen Anne Victorian style mansion located in the Sherman Heights Historic District, close to downtown San Diego. Although the interior is currently closed to visitors, the architecture alone is worth a quick visit. The haunted history has its origin in the séances held by owner Jesse Shepard, a musician of English birth. Shepard, himself, is thought to haunt the Villa, playing the piano when no one is present. Another ghost haunts the stained glass window of Peter Rubens, which has turned Rubens's beard gray over time.

Mission San Diego de Alcalá Bell Tower

The Mission Basilica San Diego de Alcalá bell tower overlooks gardens of hibiscus, succulents, olive, citrus, and avocado trees on the Mission grounds. Mission bells were an important part of early daily life, calling residents to services, meals, christenings, and funerals. They were also rung to signal the return of missionaries and ships coming into the harbor. The four-story bell tower contains five bells, one of them dating to 1802. It is the largest of the five and sports a Spanish Crown at its peak.

George W. Marston House

The Marston House was built in 1905 and is considered an outstanding example of the Arts and Crafts Movement. The 8,500-square-foot house is tucked away in a corner of the Hillcrest neighborhood at 3525 Seventh Avenue. It has five acres of formal gardens, canyonscapes, and rolling lawns. In 1987, the Marston family gifted the estate to the City of San Diego. It then became a museum administered by the Save Our Heritage Organisation (SOHO). Tours of the home and garden are offered Friday through Monday.

Unconditional Surrender

Unconditional Surrender—better known as the Kissing Statue—was sculpted by Seward Johnson and based on the iconic photo taken in Times Square on Victory in Europe (VE) Day. The much bigger-than-life-size statue is located close to the Midway Museum on the harbor. Several copies of the statue have been created and installed worldwide, including New York, Normandy, France, New Jersey, Rome, and Sarasota, Florida. Drive by the Bay and you'll often find couples beneath the statue mimicking the pose.

Casa de Balboa

The Casa de Balboa building houses several attractions including the San Diego History Center, the Model Railroad Museum, and the Museum of Photographic Arts (MOPA). The History Center sponsors several events both in the park and at the Serra Museum in Presidio Park. The 27,000-square-foot Model Railroad Museum is one of the largest of its kind. The collection includes pieces from a replica of the Atchison, Topeka, and Santa Fe lines that were built in 1935 for the California Pacific International Exposition. Visit MOPA to view photographic art spanning the decades from the 19th century to the present. Collections include works by Margaret Bourke-White and Alfred Stieglitz.

Cabrillo Statue

On September 28, 1542, Portuguese explorer Juan Rodríguez Cabrillo became the first European to sail into San Diego's protected harbor, which he named "San Miguel." A week later, Cabrillo visited Santa Catalina Island and then continued north along the California coast, exploring as far north as the Russian River. Today Cabrillo's statue overlooks San Diego's harbor and is part of Cabrillo National Monument. September 28 in California is known as Cabrillo Day. The Cabrillo National Monument is located at the tip of Point Loma. On a clear day visitors can easily see the uninhabited Coronado Islands that lie about 15 miles off the harbor's entrance.

Balboa Park

Balboa Park is a 1,200-acre green space located in the heart of San Diego. Beginning in 1909, the City decided to hold an expo in the Park to coincide with the 1915 opening of the Panama Canal. Present-day Balboa Park evolved from the exposition. The buildings for the expo were designed in a Spanish Colonial style with elaborate facades and ornamentation. The Park's second big event was the California Pacific International Exposition of 1935-1936. More buildings were added that included the Old Globe Theatre and the Spanish Village. El Prado—a wide central walkway – runs from Park Boulevard on the east, west to Laurel St. over the Cabrillo Bridge roadway.

Woman of Tehuantepec Fountain

The Woman of Tehuantepec fountain was created for the 1935-36 California Pacific International Exposition and is located in the courtyard of Balboa Park's House of Hospitality. The fountain depicts a Mayan woman holding an olla (water jar) that spills into the fountain below. The sculpture was carved by Donal Hord whose works include Guardian of the Waters which stands in front of the San Diego County Administration Building on the Bay, and Aztec (Montezuma), located at San Diego State University.

Hot Air Balloons

Most days at sunrise or sunset, look north and you'll see the sky filled with colorful hot air balloons. Several companies provide balloon rides in the county, including those in nearby Temecula that float above the vineyards and local wineries. Others provide unparalleled views of the coastline, coastal canyons, and high rises in downtown San Diego.

Hotel Del Coronado

One of San Diego's most iconic sites is the Hotel Del Coronado built in 1888. The hotel is now a National Historic Landmark. The Del is located in the City of Coronado across the bay from San Diego. It has welcomed several US Presidents as well as Prince Edward and his wife Mrs. Simpson, Charles Lindbergh, and Charlie Chaplin. Perhaps the most famous celebrity was Marilyn Monroe and the cast of "Some Like It Hot" which was filmed at the hotel. An equally famous guest, although rarely seen, is the ghost of Kate Morgan, who was an 1892 guest that committed suicide on the property.

Old Town Docent

Dedicated volunteer docents can be found at many of the historic buildings in Old Town State Historic Park. Here, a docent greets visitors to the Casa de Estudillo, which was built in 1827 by early settler José María Estudillo. The Park recreates life in early California dating from the Mexican and early American periods of 1821-1872. Three of Old Town's original adobes have been restored, which include the Casa de Estudillo, Machado y Stewart, and Machado y Silvas. The Park uses volunteers in several capacities that also include gallery guides and document archiving.

USS Midway Museum

The USS *Midway* Museum is a 20th century US Navy aircraft carrier located between the Cruise Ship Terminal and Seaport Village. Visitors can explore the vast ship from the engine room to the galleys, sleeping quarters, and 4-acre flight deck where you'll find more than 20 vintage aircraft. The hangar deck has flight simulators to challenge your flying skills, a gift shop, café, and exhibits. The self-guided audio tour, which was narrated by Midway sailors, will take you both below and above decks where you can experience life as a sailor on a real aircraft carrier.

USS Midway trainer plane image derived from photo in Creative Commons attribution
https://www.flickr.com/photos/rollercoasterphilosophy/16740998754

Old Town Blacksmith

Among Old Town's historic reenactors are several blacksmiths who ply their trade in the town's blacksmith shop that operated in the 1860s. The shop is located behind the Seeley Stables and was originally owned by J.B. Hinton. Along with blacksmithing services, Hinton also provided coach repairs and housing for horses and teamsters. Today, living history smithys perform duties authentic to the period while answering questions about their trade and the time period in which the real Old Town blacksmiths would have operated.

Lighthouse

San Diego's original lighthouse sits at the tip of Point Loma within the Cabrillo National Monument. At the time it was built in 1855, the lighthouse had the highest elevation of any in the United States. However, its location at 400-feet above sea level made it difficult for mariners to see during times of low clouds and dense fog. A new lighthouse was built in 1891 at a location below the cliffs. The lighthouse became part of the National Park Service (NPS) in 1933 but was commandeered in 1941 by the military and used as a signal tower. It was returned to the NPS after the war. Today, it remains one of San Diego's most popular attractions.

Tigers at the San Diego Zoo

Tigers are but one of the more than 650 species and sub-species that call the San Diego Zoo home. The 100-acre Zoo is located in Balboa Park, just north of Spanish Village. The Zoo is a leader in the preservation of rare and endangered wildlife. Almost all of the 3,700 animals at the Zoo are rare or endangered species. The Zoo's tiger exhibit was designed to resemble a natural jungle habitat and features a steep slope to give the big cats plenty of exercise. The Zoo's Sumatran tigers like water and enjoy swimming in their own deep pool.

Tiger image derived from photo in Creative Commons attribution
https://www.flickr.com/photos/mliu92/4317274443

The Old Globe

The Old Globe In Balboa Park was built in 1935 as part of the California Pacific International Exposition. It was built to replicate Shakespeare's Globe in London with an open center and a roof over the seating on the sides. During the year, the Old Globe is home to about 15 plays, ranging from traditional Shakespeare to works by modern playwrights. The Old Globe is one of a trio of theaters in a complex that also includes an open air theater and a theater in-the-round. The original Old Globe was destroyed by an arson's fire in 1978 and was rebuilt and opened for the 1981 theater season.

San Diego Air and Space Museum

Balboa Park's San Diego Air and Space Museum (SDASM) is a favorite of aircraft history buffs. It is one of the largest aviation museums in the country with collections spanning the history of aviation. SDASM is located in the historic Ford Building, which is on the National Register of Historic Places. In addition to the the Ford Building, the museum has two restoration facilities. Among the prized exhibitions are the Apollo 9 command module, World War I and II fighter planes, and an exact replica of Lindbergh's *Spirit of St. Louis*. Don't miss the museum's exterior where you'll find a Lockheed A-12 reconnaissance aircraft called a Blackbird.

San Diego Zoo Entrance

The world-famous San Diego Zoo is located in Balboa Park. The Zoo's origin dates to the 1915 Panama-California Exposition when exotic animals were abandoned following the closure of the expo. An agreement was reached in 1921 stating that the City would own the animals and the Zoo would serve as caretakers. Over time, the Zoo acquired animals from defunct amusement parks and became a pioneer in cageless animal enclosures. Guided bus tours cover approximately 75% of the property while the Skyfari offers an aerial view of the 100-acre Zoo.

Junípero Serra Museum

The Junípero Serra Museum located in Presidio Park is often mistaken for the Mission San Diego de Alcalá. This is not a surprise as the architect, William Templeton Johnson, chose to use a Spanish Revival style to capture the look of the old California missions. The museum was built in 1929 to house the collection of the San Diego Historical Society (now called the San Diego History Center). The museum is located only a stone's throw from the spot where Spanish Franciscan missionary Father Junípero Serra established the first mission in 1769. The museum is one of San Diego's most recognizable landmarks.

Spirit of St. Louis

The San Diego Air and Space Museum houses an exact replicate of Charles Lindbergh's record-breaking *Spirit of St. Louis*. The original Spirit was designed and built in San Diego by Ryan Airlines and today is displayed at the Smithsonian Air and Space Museum. The Spirit now on exhibit in the rotunda of San Diego's museum was built by 34 craftsmen, three of whom built the original plane. It underwent a total restoration and returned to the museum in 2006.

Safari Park

Safari Park, once known as the San Diego Wild Animal Park, is operated by the San Diego Zoo Global. The 1,800-acre wildlife sanctuary houses more than 3,000 animals and a botanical collection numbering 1.75 million specimens. The Park is located in the San Pasqual Valley near Escondido, California, and is about a 40 minute drive from downtown San Diego. Visitors can walk or take a tram to the various habitats including an Asian Savannah, African Plains, Condor Ridge, and Elephant Valley.

Heritage Park

Heritage Park is located in San Diego's Old Town. The park features several restored Victorian homes and San Diego's first synagogue—Temple Beth Israel. The historic home pictured here is the Bushyhead House, which is an Italianate style home built in 1887 that was originally owned by Edward Bushyhead. The house features tall bay windows and double doors with glass panels. Bushyhead, who was an early San Diego sheriff, was part Cherokee and marched in the infamous Trail of Tears in 1838. Other styles of homes in Heritage Park include Queen Anne, Classic Revival, and Stick Eastlake.

San Diego Natural History Museum

TheNAT, as it is known by locals, sits on the east end of El Prado in Balboa Park. Several buildings have housed the museum's collections between 1917 and 1933 when the current building was constructed. It was designed by William Templeton Johnson. The museum was commandeered by the Navy for use as an infectious disease ward during World War II and then later returned to the San Diego Society of Natural History following the war. New construction in 2001 doubled the size of the building. The museum is dedicated to interpreting the natural world through research, education, and exhibits. Exhibitions change throughout the year and have included the Dead Sea Scrolls, the Titanic, and the Discovery of King Tut.

Casa del Prado Theatre

The Casa del Prado Theatre is an historic reconstruction of a building from the 1915 Panama-California Exposition. The San Diego Civic Youth Ballet holds classes in the nearby Casa del Prado with instruction beginning at age four and continuing through pre-professional level. Aspiring young dancers perform in up to four productions each year in the Casa del Prado Theatre.

California Tower

The California Tower soars above the California Building, home to the Museum of Man. Built for the 1915 Exposition, the building has a Spanish-Colonial facade. The Tower was closed to the public in 1935, but has recently been opened, offering visitors magnificent views of San Diego. Two coats of arms can be seen on the front of the California Building, the Coat of Arms of Mexico and that of the State of California.

Gaslamp

The Gaslamp Quarter is an historical section of San Diego's downtown that is listed as an historic district on the National Register of Historic Places. Home to music festivals, upscale bars, and restaurants, the Gaslamp claims 94 historic buildings. In the last two decades of the 19th century, the Gaslamp was known as the Stingaree, hosting a multitude of saloons, bordellos, and gambling halls. A century later, it became the focus of a major redevelopment leading to the trendy neighborhood that you see today.

Jewish Temple

The original Temple Beth Israel is located in Old Town's Heritage Park. It was the first Jewish temple in San Diego and one of the oldest synagogue buildings in the American west. Originally built at the corner of Second and Beech Streets in downtown San Diego, the temple was used until 1926, at which time the congregation moved to a larger building at Third and Laurel Streets. According to the late historian Henry Schwartz, Jewish pioneers arrived in San Diego in 1850, first meeting in 1861 to form the congregation that eventually became Beth Israel.

Sunbelt Publications Recommended Reading

Coast to Cactus: The Canyoneer Trail Guide to San Diego Outdoors Diana Lindsay, Managing Ed.
Take a hike with a naturalist—a virtual Canyoneer to know and appreciate San Diego County's biodiversity while exploring it firsthand with any one of over 250 trail guides, written by the San Diego Natural History Museum Canyoneers.

La Jolla: A Photographic Journey Nick Agelidis
Stunning photographs depict the beauty and charm of La Jolla that show why this seaside village has been the destination of world travelers since the 1880s.

My Ancestors' Village Roberta Labastida
This charming story told from the view point of a young Indian from the Kumeyaay (Kumiai) nation, describes the traditional way a family lived in earlier times in the countryside of the Alta/Baja California borderlands.

San Diego: An Introduction to the Region, 5th edition . Philip Pryde
This is the essential one-volume reference to the history, economics, demographics, natural features, and environmental issues of today's binational region on the Pacific borderlands, home to Native Americans for millennia with an insightful overview of "The County's First Residents."

San Diego Legends, 2nd edition Jack Innis
San Diego journalist Jack Innis describes the many fascinating people and events that influenced the development of San Diego, plus the colorful characters and groups that made headlines in the past century.

San Diego Specters John Lamb
Only the most authentic and plausible ghostly tales are included in this entertaining investigation into famous and obscure haunted sites throughout San Diego County.

San Diego: California's Cornerstone, 2nd Edition Iris Engstrand
This work is a sweeping history of the region from the time of its indigenous people to the 21st c. Chapters cover the Spanish, Mexican, Victorian, WWI and WWII eras and the postwar boom, up to Petco Park and the 2004 mayoral election. Includes a chronology of events, bibliography, and index.

Panda Who Would Not Eat Ruth Todd Evans
The true story of a panda at the San Diego Zoo who refuses to eat until…? (Answer in this book!)

Tom Hom, Rabbit on a Bumpy Road: A Story of Courage and Endurance Tom Hom
This is Tom's memoir in meeting life's challenges to achieve "The American Dream." He was born into a Chinese family in the year of the Rabbit in the 1920's when much of American society was segregated, socially and economically. He never lost faith in the American dream and went on to achieve success for himself, his family, and the greater good of a diverse America. Today, Tom Hom is a respected elder who has inspired a new generation of Americans. His journey and words of wisdom offer encouragement to all who believe in the future of America.

Sunbelt produces and distributes publications about "Adventures in the Natural History and Cultural Heritage of the Californias" including guidebooks, regional references, pictorials, and stories that celebrate the land and its people.